40 Avocado Recipes for Home

By: Kelly Johnson

Table of Contents

Appetizers and Snacks:

- Avocado Bruschetta
- Guacamole
- Avocado Hummus
- Avocado Egg Rolls
- Avocado Salsa
- Spicy Avocado Deviled Eggs
- Avocado Fries
- Avocado and Shrimp Ceviche

Salads:

- Caprese Avocado Salad
- Cobb Salad with Avocado Ranch Dressing
- Avocado and Quinoa Salad
- Mango Avocado Salad

Main Dishes:

- Grilled Avocado Chicken
- Avocado and Black Bean Quesadillas
- Avocado Pesto Pasta
- Avocado and Tuna Stuffed Bell Peppers
- Avocado and Chickpea Wrap

Sandwiches and Burgers:

- Turkey and Avocado Club Sandwich
- Avocado BLT
- Chicken Avocado Burger
- Vegetarian Avocado Panini

Soups and Stews:

- Chilled Avocado Soup
- Chicken Avocado Lime Soup

- Black Bean and Avocado Chili
- Avocado and Corn Chowder

Breakfast and Brunch:

- Avocado Toast Variations
- Avocado and Spinach Omelette
- Avocado Pancakes
- Breakfast Burrito with Avocado

Dressings and Sauces:

- Creamy Avocado Caesar Dressing
- Avocado Chimichurri Sauce
- Avocado Lime Crema

Desserts:

- Avocado Chocolate Mousse
- Avocado Lime Cheesecake Bars
- Avocado Key Lime Pie
- Avocado Coconut Ice Cream

Drinks:

- Avocado Smoothie
- Avocado Margarita
- Avocado Matcha Latte
- Avocado and Berry Smoothie Bowl

Appetizers and Snacks:

Avocado Bruschetta

Ingredients:

- Baguette slices or crostini
- 2 ripe avocados, peeled, pitted, and diced
- 1 cup cherry tomatoes, diced
- 1/4 cup red onion, finely chopped
- 2 cloves garlic, minced
- 1/4 cup fresh basil, chopped
- 2 tablespoons balsamic glaze
- 2 tablespoons extra-virgin olive oil
- Salt and black pepper to taste

Instructions:

Prepare Baguette Slices:
- Preheat the oven or toaster oven. Slice the baguette into 1/2-inch thick rounds. Toast the slices until they are golden brown and crisp.

Prepare Avocado Mixture:
- In a bowl, combine diced avocados, cherry tomatoes, red onion, minced garlic, and chopped basil.

Season:
- Drizzle extra-virgin olive oil over the avocado mixture. Add salt and black pepper to taste. Gently toss to combine.

Assemble Bruschetta:
- Spoon the avocado mixture onto each toasted baguette slice.

Drizzle with Balsamic Glaze:
- Drizzle balsamic glaze over the avocado bruschetta for a sweet and tangy finish.

Serve:
- Arrange the Avocado Bruschetta on a serving platter. Serve immediately as a delightful appetizer or snack.

This Avocado Bruschetta is a refreshing twist on the classic tomato bruschetta, adding the creamy and nutritious goodness of ripe avocados. It's a perfect starter for any gathering, offering a burst of flavors and textures with each bite. Enjoy!

Guacamole

Ingredients:

- 3 ripe avocados
- 1 small red onion, finely diced
- 1-2 tomatoes, diced
- 1/4 cup fresh cilantro, chopped
- 1-2 cloves garlic, minced
- 1 lime, juiced
- Salt and black pepper to taste
- Optional: Jalapeño, finely chopped, for heat

Instructions:

Prepare Avocados:
- Cut the avocados in half, remove the pits, and scoop the flesh into a mixing bowl.

Mash Avocados:
- Mash the avocados using a fork or potato masher until you achieve your desired level of smoothness.

Add Vegetables:
- Add the finely diced red onion, diced tomatoes, minced garlic, and chopped cilantro to the mashed avocados.

Season:
- Squeeze the juice of one lime into the mixture. Season with salt and black pepper to taste.

Optional Heat:
- If you like a spicy guacamole, add finely chopped jalapeño to the mixture.

Mix Well:
- Gently fold all the ingredients together until well combined.

Taste and Adjust:
- Taste the guacamole and adjust the seasoning, adding more salt, pepper, or lime juice if needed.

Chill (Optional):
- For enhanced flavor, refrigerate the guacamole for at least 30 minutes before serving.

Serve:

- Transfer the guacamole to a serving bowl. Garnish with additional cilantro. Serve with tortilla chips or as a topping for tacos, nachos, or your favorite dishes.

This Classic Guacamole recipe is a crowd-pleaser, offering a perfect balance of creamy avocados, fresh vegetables, and zesty lime juice. It's a versatile dip that adds a burst of flavor to various meals and snacks. Enjoy the delicious simplicity of homemade guacamole!

Avocado Hummus

Ingredients:

- 1 can (15 oz) chickpeas, drained and rinsed
- 2 ripe avocados, peeled and pitted
- 3 tablespoons tahini
- 3 tablespoons olive oil
- 2 cloves garlic, minced
- 1 teaspoon ground cumin
- 1/2 teaspoon paprika
- Juice of 1 lemon
- Salt and black pepper to taste
- Optional toppings: olive oil, chopped cilantro, and red pepper flakes

Instructions:

Prepare Chickpeas:
- Drain and rinse the chickpeas under cold water.

Combine Ingredients:
- In a food processor, combine chickpeas, ripe avocados, tahini, olive oil, minced garlic, ground cumin, paprika, and lemon juice.

Blend:
- Process the mixture until smooth and creamy. If needed, scrape down the sides of the food processor to ensure all ingredients are well incorporated.

Season:
- Season the avocado hummus with salt and black pepper to taste. Adjust the seasoning as needed.

Serve:
- Transfer the avocado hummus to a serving bowl.

Optional Toppings:
- Drizzle with olive oil and sprinkle chopped cilantro and red pepper flakes on top for added flavor and presentation.

Chill (Optional):
- Refrigerate the avocado hummus for at least 30 minutes before serving for a cool and refreshing dip.

Serve:
- Serve the avocado hummus with pita bread, veggie sticks, or as a spread on sandwiches and wraps.

This Avocado Hummus is a creamy and flavorful twist on traditional hummus. The addition of ripe avocados brings a smooth texture and a subtle, buttery taste. It's a perfect dip for any occasion and a delicious way to enjoy the goodness of avocados. Enjoy!

Avocado Egg Rolls

Ingredients:

For the Filling:

- 2 ripe avocados, peeled, pitted, and diced
- 1 cup red cabbage, thinly shredded
- 1 cup carrots, julienned
- 1/4 cup red bell pepper, thinly sliced
- 2 green onions, thinly sliced
- 1/4 cup cilantro, chopped
- 1 tablespoon soy sauce
- 1 teaspoon sesame oil
- 1 teaspoon rice vinegar
- 1 teaspoon fresh ginger, grated
- 1 clove garlic, minced
- 1 tablespoon lime juice

For Rolling:

- Egg roll wrappers
- Water (for sealing)

For Frying:

- Vegetable oil (for frying)

For Dipping Sauce:

- 1/4 cup soy sauce
- 1 tablespoon rice vinegar
- 1 teaspoon sesame oil
- 1 teaspoon honey
- 1 teaspoon sriracha (optional, for heat)

Instructions:

    Prepare Avocado Mixture:

- In a large bowl, combine diced avocados, shredded red cabbage, julienned carrots, sliced red bell pepper, sliced green onions, and chopped cilantro.

Make Sauce:
- In a small bowl, whisk together soy sauce, sesame oil, rice vinegar, grated ginger, minced garlic, and lime juice. Pour the sauce over the avocado mixture and toss until well combined.

Prepare Rolling Station:
- Lay an egg roll wrapper on a clean surface with one corner pointing towards you. Place a spoonful of the avocado mixture in the center of the wrapper.

Roll and Seal:
- Fold the corner closest to you over the filling, then fold in the sides. Roll the wrapper away from you, sealing the edge with water. Ensure the egg roll is tightly sealed.

Repeat:
- Repeat the process with the remaining wrappers and filling.

Heat Oil:
- In a deep skillet or pot, heat vegetable oil to 350°F (175°C).

Fry Egg Rolls:
- Carefully place a few egg rolls into the hot oil and fry until golden brown, turning occasionally for even cooking. Remove with a slotted spoon and place on a paper towel-lined plate to drain excess oil.

Make Dipping Sauce:
- In a small bowl, mix together soy sauce, rice vinegar, sesame oil, honey, and sriracha (if using).

Serve:
- Serve the Avocado Egg Rolls hot with the dipping sauce on the side.

These Avocado Egg Rolls are a crispy and delightful appetizer with a creamy avocado filling. The combination of textures and flavors makes them a crowd-pleaser, and the dipping sauce adds an extra layer of deliciousness. Enjoy!

Avocado Salsa

Ingredients:

- 3 ripe avocados, diced
- 1 cup cherry tomatoes, diced
- 1/2 red onion, finely chopped
- 1/4 cup fresh cilantro, chopped
- 1 jalapeño, seeds removed and finely chopped
- 2 cloves garlic, minced
- Juice of 2 limes
- Salt and black pepper to taste
- Optional: 1 teaspoon cumin powder

Instructions:

Prepare Ingredients:
- Dice the avocados, cherry tomatoes, and red onion. Finely chop the cilantro and jalapeño. Mince the garlic.

Combine Ingredients:
- In a large bowl, combine the diced avocados, cherry tomatoes, red onion, cilantro, jalapeño, and minced garlic.

Season:
- Squeeze the juice of two limes over the ingredients. Add salt and black pepper to taste. If desired, sprinkle cumin powder for additional flavor.

Gently Toss:
- Gently toss the ingredients together until well combined. Be careful not to mash the avocados completely, leaving some chunks for texture.

Chill (Optional):
- For enhanced flavor, refrigerate the Avocado Salsa for at least 30 minutes before serving.

Adjust Seasoning:
- Taste the salsa and adjust the seasoning if needed, adding more lime juice, salt, or pepper according to your preference.

Serve:
- Transfer the Avocado Salsa to a serving bowl. Serve with tortilla chips, as a topping for grilled chicken or fish, or as a refreshing side dish.

This Avocado Salsa is a vibrant and flavorful combination of fresh ingredients. It's perfect for dipping or as a topping to add a burst of color and taste to your favorite dishes. Enjoy the creamy goodness of avocados in this delicious salsa!

Spicy Avocado Deviled Eggs

Ingredients:

- 6 large eggs, hard-boiled and peeled
- 2 ripe avocados, peeled and pitted
- 1 tablespoon mayonnaise
- 1 tablespoon Dijon mustard
- 1 tablespoon lime juice
- 1 jalapeño, finely chopped (seeds removed for less heat, if desired)
- 1/4 cup red onion, finely chopped
- Salt and black pepper to taste
- Paprika or chili powder for garnish

Instructions:

Prepare Hard-Boiled Eggs:
- Hard-boil the eggs, then cool, peel, and cut them in half lengthwise. Remove the yolks and set aside.

Make Avocado Filling:
- In a bowl, mash the ripe avocados until smooth.

Prepare Deviled Egg Filling:
- Add the egg yolks to the mashed avocados. Add mayonnaise, Dijon mustard, lime juice, chopped jalapeño, and chopped red onion.

Season:
- Season the mixture with salt and black pepper to taste. Adjust the spice level by adding more jalapeño if desired.

Mix Thoroughly:
- Mix the ingredients until well combined and creamy. You can use a fork or a hand mixer for a smoother consistency.

Fill Egg Whites:
- Spoon or pipe the avocado deviled egg filling into the hollowed egg whites.

Garnish:
- Sprinkle paprika or chili powder over the filled eggs for a touch of color and additional spice.

Chill (Optional):
- For enhanced flavor, refrigerate the Spicy Avocado Deviled Eggs for at least 30 minutes before serving.

Serve:
- Arrange the deviled eggs on a serving platter and serve as a spicy and creamy appetizer or snack.

These Spicy Avocado Deviled Eggs are a unique and flavorful twist on the classic recipe. The combination of creamy avocado and a kick of spice from jalapeño adds a delicious dimension to this popular appetizer. Enjoy the bold flavors in every bite!

Avocado Fries

Ingredients:

- 2 large avocados, firm and ripe
- 1 cup breadcrumbs (panko works well)
- 1/2 cup all-purpose flour
- 2 large eggs, beaten
- 1 teaspoon garlic powder
- 1 teaspoon paprika
- Salt and black pepper to taste
- Cooking spray or vegetable oil for baking

Instructions:

Preheat Oven:
- Preheat your oven to 425°F (220°C).

Prepare Avocado:
- Cut the avocados in half, remove the pit, and carefully peel each half. Cut the peeled avocados into thick slices.

Set Up Coating Station:
- In three separate bowls, place the flour in one, beaten eggs in another, and breadcrumbs mixed with garlic powder, paprika, salt, and black pepper in the third.

Coat Avocado Slices:
- Dip each avocado slice into the flour, shaking off excess. Then dip it into the beaten eggs, ensuring it's coated evenly. Finally, coat it in the breadcrumb mixture, pressing the breadcrumbs onto the avocado to adhere.

Place on Baking Sheet:
- Arrange the coated avocado slices on a baking sheet lined with parchment paper. Ensure they are evenly spaced and not touching.

Bake:
- Lightly spray the avocado fries with cooking spray or drizzle with vegetable oil. Bake in the preheated oven for 12-15 minutes or until the fries are golden and crispy, flipping them halfway through for even cooking.

Cool Slightly:
- Allow the avocado fries to cool slightly before serving.

Serve:
- Serve the Avocado Fries warm as a delicious appetizer or snack. They pair well with your favorite dipping sauce, such as ranch, aioli, or salsa.

These Avocado Fries are a healthier alternative to traditional fries, offering a crispy exterior and creamy interior. They make for a delightful and unique snack or side dish, perfect for any occasion. Enjoy the deliciousness of avocados in a new and exciting form!

Avocado and Shrimp Ceviche

Ingredients:

- 1 pound medium shrimp, peeled, deveined, and cooked
- 3 ripe avocados, diced
- 1 cup cherry tomatoes, halved
- 1/2 red onion, finely chopped
- 1 cucumber, peeled and diced
- 1 jalapeño, seeds removed and finely chopped
- 1/2 cup fresh cilantro, chopped
- Juice of 4-5 limes
- Juice of 1 orange
- Salt and black pepper to taste
- Tortilla chips for serving

Instructions:

Prepare Shrimp:
- Cook the shrimp in boiling water until they turn pink and opaque. Drain, cool, and chop into bite-sized pieces.

Combine Ingredients:
- In a large bowl, combine the cooked shrimp, diced avocados, halved cherry tomatoes, finely chopped red onion, diced cucumber, chopped jalapeño, and chopped cilantro.

Citrus Juices:
- Squeeze the juice of 4-5 limes and the juice of 1 orange over the mixture. Adjust the amount of citrus juice to your taste preference.

Season:
- Season the ceviche with salt and black pepper to taste. Gently toss the ingredients to combine.

Chill:
- Cover the bowl with plastic wrap and refrigerate the ceviche for at least 30 minutes to allow the flavors to meld.

Serve:
- Serve the Avocado and Shrimp Ceviche in individual bowls or glasses. Optionally, garnish with additional cilantro.

Enjoy:
- Enjoy the ceviche with tortilla chips for scooping. It's a refreshing and flavorful appetizer or light meal.

This Avocado and Shrimp Ceviche is a light and zesty dish that combines the creaminess of avocados with the freshness of shrimp and citrus. It's perfect for warm days or as a starter for a festive gathering. Delight in the vibrant flavors of this classic ceviche!

Salads:

Caprese Avocado Salad

Ingredients:

- 3 ripe avocados, sliced
- 3 large tomatoes, sliced
- 1 pound fresh mozzarella cheese, sliced
- Fresh basil leaves
- Balsamic glaze, for drizzling
- Extra-virgin olive oil, for drizzling
- Salt and black pepper to taste

Instructions:

Prepare Ingredients:
- Slice the avocados, tomatoes, and fresh mozzarella into even, round slices.

Arrange on a Platter:
- Alternately layer the avocado slices, tomato slices, and mozzarella slices on a serving platter.

Add Basil Leaves:
- Tuck fresh basil leaves between the slices of avocado, tomato, and mozzarella.

Season:
- Sprinkle salt and black pepper over the salad to taste.

Drizzle with Olive Oil:
- Drizzle extra-virgin olive oil over the layered salad for richness.

Balsamic Glaze:
- Finish by drizzling balsamic glaze over the Caprese Avocado Salad for a sweet and tangy touch.

Serve:
- Serve the salad immediately as a refreshing and visually appealing appetizer or side dish.

This Caprese Avocado Salad is a delightful twist on the classic Caprese salad, incorporating creamy avocados for an extra layer of flavor and texture. It's a simple and elegant dish that showcases the beauty of fresh, high-quality ingredients. Enjoy the combination of ripe avocados, juicy tomatoes, and creamy mozzarella in every bite!

Cobb Salad with Avocado Ranch Dressing

Ingredients:

For the Salad:

- 4 cups mixed salad greens (e.g., romaine lettuce, arugula)
- 2 cups cooked and diced chicken breast
- 6 strips bacon, cooked and crumbled
- 2 hard-boiled eggs, sliced
- 1 cup cherry tomatoes, halved
- 1 avocado, diced
- 1/2 cup crumbled blue cheese
- 1/4 cup sliced green onions

For the Avocado Ranch Dressing:

- 1 ripe avocado, peeled and pitted
- 1/2 cup plain Greek yogurt
- 1/4 cup mayonnaise
- 1 clove garlic, minced
- 2 tablespoons fresh parsley, chopped
- 2 tablespoons fresh chives, chopped
- 1 tablespoon fresh dill, chopped
- Juice of 1 lemon
- Salt and black pepper to taste
- Water (as needed to thin the dressing)

Instructions:

Prepare Avocado Ranch Dressing:
- In a blender or food processor, combine the ripe avocado, Greek yogurt, mayonnaise, minced garlic, fresh parsley, fresh chives, fresh dill, and lemon juice. Blend until smooth.
- Season the dressing with salt and black pepper to taste. If the dressing is too thick, add water, a tablespoon at a time, until it reaches your desired consistency.

Assemble Salad:
- In a large salad bowl or on individual plates, arrange the mixed salad greens.

- Top the greens with diced chicken breast, crumbled bacon, sliced hard-boiled eggs, cherry tomatoes, diced avocado, crumbled blue cheese, and sliced green onions.

Serve with Dressing:
- Drizzle the Avocado Ranch Dressing generously over the Cobb Salad.

Toss or Serve As Is:
- Toss the salad gently to coat all ingredients in the dressing or serve as is for a visually appealing presentation.

Enjoy:
- Serve the Cobb Salad with Avocado Ranch Dressing immediately as a hearty and flavorful meal.

This Cobb Salad with Avocado Ranch Dressing combines the classic Cobb salad ingredients with a creamy and flavorful avocado-based ranch dressing. It's a satisfying and nutritious meal that's perfect for lunch or dinner. Enjoy the vibrant colors and delicious taste of this well-balanced salad!

Avocado and Quinoa Salad

Ingredients:

For the Salad:

- 1 cup quinoa, rinsed
- 2 cups water
- 2 ripe avocados, diced
- 1 cup cherry tomatoes, halved
- 1 cucumber, diced
- 1/4 cup red onion, finely chopped
- 1/4 cup fresh cilantro, chopped
- 1/4 cup feta cheese, crumbled (optional)
- Salt and black pepper to taste

For the Dressing:

- 3 tablespoons extra-virgin olive oil
- 2 tablespoons balsamic vinegar
- 1 tablespoon lime juice
- 1 teaspoon Dijon mustard
- 1 clove garlic, minced
- Salt and black pepper to taste

Instructions:

Cook Quinoa:
- In a medium saucepan, combine quinoa and water. Bring to a boil, then reduce heat to low, cover, and simmer for 15-20 minutes or until quinoa is cooked and water is absorbed. Fluff the quinoa with a fork and let it cool.

Prepare Dressing:
- In a small bowl, whisk together olive oil, balsamic vinegar, lime juice, Dijon mustard, minced garlic, salt, and black pepper. Set aside.

Assemble Salad:
- In a large salad bowl, combine the cooked and cooled quinoa with diced avocados, halved cherry tomatoes, diced cucumber, finely chopped red onion, chopped cilantro, and crumbled feta cheese (if using).

Drizzle Dressing:
- Drizzle the prepared dressing over the salad ingredients.

Toss Gently:

- Gently toss the salad until all ingredients are well coated with the dressing.

Season:
- Season the salad with additional salt and black pepper to taste.

Chill (Optional):
- For enhanced flavor, refrigerate the Avocado and Quinoa Salad for at least 30 minutes before serving.

Serve:
- Serve the salad chilled as a refreshing and nutritious side dish or a light meal.

This Avocado and Quinoa Salad is a nutritious and flavorful option that combines the goodness of quinoa and avocados. The balsamic-lime dressing adds a zesty kick, making it a perfect dish for lunch or as a side at your next gathering. Enjoy the satisfying textures and vibrant colors in each bite!

Mango Avocado Salad

Ingredients:

For the Salad:

- 2 ripe avocados, diced
- 2 ripe mangoes, peeled, pitted, and diced
- 1 cup cherry tomatoes, halved
- 1/2 cucumber, diced
- 1/4 cup red onion, finely chopped
- 1/4 cup fresh cilantro, chopped
- 1/4 cup feta cheese, crumbled (optional)
- 1/4 cup almonds, sliced or chopped
- Mixed salad greens (optional)

For the Dressing:

- 3 tablespoons extra-virgin olive oil
- 2 tablespoons balsamic vinegar
- 1 tablespoon honey
- 1 teaspoon Dijon mustard
- Salt and black pepper to taste

Instructions:

Prepare Dressing:
- In a small bowl, whisk together olive oil, balsamic vinegar, honey, Dijon mustard, salt, and black pepper. Set aside.

Assemble Salad:
- In a large salad bowl, combine diced avocados, diced mangoes, halved cherry tomatoes, diced cucumber, finely chopped red onion, chopped cilantro, crumbled feta cheese (if using), and sliced almonds.

Optional Greens:
- If desired, you can serve the salad on a bed of mixed salad greens for added freshness.

Drizzle Dressing:
- Drizzle the prepared dressing over the salad ingredients.

Toss Gently:
- Gently toss the salad until all ingredients are well coated with the dressing.

Season:
- Season the salad with additional salt and black pepper to taste.

Chill (Optional):
- For enhanced flavor, refrigerate the Mango Avocado Salad for at least 30 minutes before serving.

Serve:
- Serve the salad chilled as a refreshing and tropical side dish or a light meal.

This Mango Avocado Salad is a vibrant and tropical dish that combines the sweetness of mangoes with the creamy texture of avocados. The honey-balsamic dressing adds a delightful sweetness, making it a perfect choice for a summer salad. Enjoy the burst of flavors and colors in each bite!

Main Dishes:

Grilled Avocado Chicken

Ingredients:

- 4 boneless, skinless chicken breasts
- 2 ripe avocados, sliced
- 1 lime, juiced
- 2 cloves garlic, minced
- 2 tablespoons olive oil
- 1 teaspoon ground cumin
- 1 teaspoon paprika
- Salt and black pepper to taste
- Fresh cilantro, chopped (for garnish)
- Lime wedges (for serving)

Instructions:

Marinate Chicken:
- In a bowl, combine lime juice, minced garlic, olive oil, ground cumin, paprika, salt, and black pepper. Place the chicken breasts in a resealable plastic bag and pour half of the marinade over them. Seal the bag and refrigerate for at least 30 minutes to marinate.

Preheat Grill:
- Preheat the grill to medium-high heat.

Grill Chicken:
- Remove the chicken from the marinade and grill for 6-8 minutes per side or until the internal temperature reaches 165°F (74°C) and the chicken is fully cooked.

Grill Avocado:
- During the last 2-3 minutes of grilling, place avocado slices on the grill and cook briefly on each side until grill marks appear.

Assemble Dish:
- Arrange the grilled chicken breasts on a serving platter. Top each chicken breast with grilled avocado slices.

Garnish:
- Drizzle the remaining marinade over the grilled avocado chicken. Garnish with fresh chopped cilantro.

Serve:
- Serve the Grilled Avocado Chicken with lime wedges on the side. It pairs well with rice, quinoa, or a side salad.

Enjoy:
- Enjoy this flavorful and healthy grilled dish with the combination of tender chicken and creamy grilled avocados.

This Grilled Avocado Chicken recipe combines the smoky goodness of grilled chicken with the creamy texture of avocados. The marinade adds a burst of flavor, making it a delicious and satisfying dish for your next barbecue or dinner. Enjoy the unique combination of grilled goodness!

Avocado and Black Bean Quesadillas

Ingredients:

- 4 large flour tortillas
- 2 ripe avocados, peeled, pitted, and sliced
- 1 can (15 oz) black beans, drained and rinsed
- 1 cup corn kernels (fresh, frozen, or canned)
- 1 cup shredded Monterey Jack or Mexican blend cheese
- 1/2 cup red onion, finely chopped
- 1/4 cup fresh cilantro, chopped
- 1 teaspoon ground cumin
- 1 teaspoon chili powder
- Salt and black pepper to taste
- Cooking spray or vegetable oil for cooking
- Salsa, sour cream, or guacamole (for serving, optional)

Instructions:

Prepare Filling:
- In a bowl, combine black beans, corn, red onion, ground cumin, chili powder, salt, and black pepper. Mix well.

Assemble Quesadillas:
- Lay out the flour tortillas on a clean surface. On one half of each tortilla, layer sliced avocados, the black bean and corn mixture, shredded cheese, and chopped cilantro.

Fold and Seal:
- Fold the tortillas in half to cover the filling, creating a half-moon shape. Press down gently to seal the edges.

Cook Quesadillas:
- Heat a large skillet or griddle over medium heat. Spray with cooking spray or brush with vegetable oil.
- Cook each quesadilla for 2-3 minutes per side, or until the tortilla is golden brown, and the cheese is melted.

Slice:
- Remove the quesadillas from the skillet and let them rest for a minute. Use a sharp knife or pizza cutter to slice each quesadilla into wedges.

Serve:
- Serve the Avocado and Black Bean Quesadillas warm with salsa, sour cream, or guacamole on the side if desired.

Enjoy:
- Enjoy these delicious quesadillas as a quick and flavorful meal. They make for a satisfying lunch or dinner option.

These Avocado and Black Bean Quesadillas are a tasty and nutritious option for a quick meal. The combination of creamy avocados, savory black beans, and melted cheese creates a satisfying flavor profile. Customize with your favorite toppings and enjoy the goodness in every bite!

Avocado Pesto Pasta

Ingredients:

- 12 oz (340g) pasta of your choice (e.g., spaghetti, fettuccine)
- 2 ripe avocados, peeled and pitted
- 1 cup fresh basil leaves, packed
- 1/2 cup grated Parmesan cheese
- 1/4 cup pine nuts
- 2 cloves garlic, minced
- 1/2 cup extra-virgin olive oil
- Juice of 1 lemon
- Salt and black pepper to taste
- Cherry tomatoes, halved (for garnish, optional)
- Extra Parmesan cheese (for serving, optional)

Instructions:

Cook Pasta:
- Cook the pasta according to the package instructions. Drain and set aside.

Prepare Avocado Pesto:
- In a food processor, combine ripe avocados, fresh basil leaves, grated Parmesan cheese, pine nuts, minced garlic, olive oil, lemon juice, salt, and black pepper.

Blend:
- Blend the ingredients until the mixture is smooth and well combined. If needed, scrape down the sides of the food processor to ensure everything is incorporated.

Toss with Pasta:
- In a large mixing bowl, toss the cooked pasta with the avocado pesto sauce until the pasta is evenly coated.

Adjust Seasoning:
- Taste and adjust the seasoning, adding more salt, pepper, or lemon juice if desired.

Serve:
- Transfer the Avocado Pesto Pasta to serving plates. Garnish with halved cherry tomatoes and extra Parmesan cheese if desired.

Enjoy:
- Enjoy this creamy and flavorful Avocado Pesto Pasta as a delicious and satisfying meal.

This Avocado Pesto Pasta is a refreshing twist on traditional pesto pasta, incorporating creamy avocados for a rich and luscious sauce. The combination of fresh basil, garlic, and Parmesan creates a delightful flavor that pairs perfectly with the smooth texture of avocados. It's a quick and easy dish for avocado lovers!

Avocado and Tuna Stuffed Bell Peppers

Ingredients:

- 4 large bell peppers, halved and seeds removed
- 2 cans (5 oz each) tuna, drained
- 2 ripe avocados, peeled, pitted, and diced
- 1/2 red onion, finely chopped
- 1 celery stalk, finely chopped
- 1/4 cup fresh cilantro, chopped
- 1 tablespoon Dijon mustard
- 1 tablespoon mayonnaise
- Juice of 1 lime
- Salt and black pepper to taste
- 1 cup cherry tomatoes, halved (for garnish, optional)
- Fresh parsley or cilantro leaves (for garnish, optional)

Instructions:

Preheat Oven:
- Preheat the oven to 375°F (190°C).

Prepare Bell Peppers:
- Cut the bell peppers in half lengthwise, removing the seeds and membranes. Place the pepper halves in a baking dish.

Make Filling:
- In a bowl, combine drained tuna, diced avocados, finely chopped red onion, chopped celery, chopped cilantro, Dijon mustard, mayonnaise, lime juice, salt, and black pepper. Mix well.

Stuff Peppers:
- Spoon the tuna and avocado mixture into each bell pepper half, pressing down gently to pack the filling.

Bake:
- Bake in the preheated oven for 20-25 minutes or until the peppers are tender.

Garnish (Optional):
- Garnish the stuffed peppers with halved cherry tomatoes and fresh parsley or cilantro leaves if desired.

Serve:
- Serve the Avocado and Tuna Stuffed Bell Peppers warm as a wholesome and flavorful dish.

Enjoy:

- Enjoy this nutritious and protein-packed meal with the combination of tuna, creamy avocados, and fresh vegetables.

These Avocado and Tuna Stuffed Bell Peppers are a delicious and healthy option for a light meal or appetizer. Packed with protein and nutrients, this dish combines the flavors of tuna and creamy avocados for a satisfying and flavorful experience. Enjoy the vibrant colors and wholesome ingredients in every bite!

Avocado and Chickpea Wrap

Ingredients:

- 1 can (15 oz) chickpeas, drained and rinsed
- 1 ripe avocado, peeled, pitted, and sliced
- 1 cup cherry tomatoes, halved
- 1/2 red onion, thinly sliced
- 1/4 cup fresh cilantro, chopped
- Juice of 1 lime
- 1 teaspoon ground cumin
- 1 teaspoon paprika
- Salt and black pepper to taste
- 4 whole-grain or spinach tortillas
- Greek yogurt or tzatziki sauce (for dressing, optional)

Instructions:

Prepare Chickpea Mixture:
- In a bowl, combine chickpeas, sliced avocado, halved cherry tomatoes, thinly sliced red onion, chopped cilantro, lime juice, ground cumin, paprika, salt, and black pepper. Gently toss to mix the ingredients.

Warm Tortillas:
- Warm the tortillas in a dry skillet or microwave according to the package instructions.

Assemble Wraps:
- Spoon the chickpea and avocado mixture onto the center of each tortilla.

Fold and Roll:
- Fold the sides of the tortilla towards the center and then roll it up tightly from the bottom to form a wrap.

Serve:
- Serve the Avocado and Chickpea Wraps as a delicious and portable meal.

Optional Dressing:
- If desired, drizzle Greek yogurt or tzatziki sauce over the chickpea mixture before folding the wraps for added creaminess.

Enjoy:
- Enjoy these flavorful and nutrient-packed wraps for a quick and satisfying lunch or dinner.

These Avocado and Chickpea Wraps are a quick and nutritious meal option. The combination of creamy avocado, protein-rich chickpeas, and fresh vegetables creates a tasty and filling wrap.

Customize with your favorite dressing and herbs for added flavor. Enjoy this simple and wholesome dish!

Sandwiches and Burgers:

Turkey and Avocado Club Sandwich

Ingredients:

- 8 slices whole grain bread
- 1 pound (about 450g) roasted turkey breast, sliced
- 8 slices bacon, cooked
- 1 large ripe avocado, peeled, pitted, and sliced
- 1 large tomato, sliced
- 4 lettuce leaves
- Mayonnaise (optional)
- Mustard (optional)
- Salt and black pepper to taste

Instructions:

    Prepare Ingredients:
- Cook bacon until crispy. Slice the roasted turkey, peel and pit the avocado, slice the tomato, and wash the lettuce leaves.

    Toast Bread:
- Toast the slices of whole grain bread until they reach your desired level of crispiness.

    Assemble First Layer:
- Lay out four slices of toasted bread. If desired, spread a thin layer of mayonnaise and/or mustard on each slice.

    Layer Turkey and Bacon:
- Place a layer of sliced roasted turkey on two of the bread slices. Add a few slices of bacon on top.

    Add Avocado and Tomato:
- Add slices of ripe avocado and tomato on the other two bread slices.

    Season and Add Lettuce:
- Sprinkle salt and black pepper to taste on the avocado and tomato slices. Place a lettuce leaf on each.

    Assemble Second Layer:
- Carefully stack the slices with turkey and bacon on top of the slices with avocado and tomato, creating two double-layered sandwiches.

    Slice and Serve:

- Use a sharp knife to slice each sandwich diagonally, creating triangular halves. Secure each half with toothpicks if needed.

Enjoy:
- Serve the Turkey and Avocado Club Sandwiches immediately. They make for a satisfying and flavorful meal.

This Turkey and Avocado Club Sandwich is a classic and delicious option for a hearty lunch or dinner. The combination of roasted turkey, crispy bacon, creamy avocado, and fresh vegetables creates a well-balanced and flavorful sandwich. Enjoy this club sandwich as a substantial and satisfying meal!

Avocado BLT

Ingredients:

- 4 slices whole grain bread
- 8 slices bacon, cooked until crispy
- 1 large ripe avocado, peeled, pitted, and sliced
- 1 large tomato, sliced
- Lettuce leaves (e.g., Romaine or iceberg)
- Mayonnaise
- Salt and black pepper to taste

Instructions:

Prepare Ingredients:
- Cook the bacon until it reaches a crispy texture. Slice the ripe avocado and tomato.

Toast Bread (Optional):
- Toast the slices of whole grain bread if desired.

Spread Mayonnaise:
- Spread a generous layer of mayonnaise on one side of each slice of bread.

Assemble Sandwich:
- On one slice of bread, layer lettuce leaves, followed by slices of crispy bacon, avocado slices, and tomato slices.

Season:
- Sprinkle salt and black pepper to taste over the avocado and tomato.

Top with Another Slice:
- Place another slice of bread on top, mayo side down.

Slice and Serve:
- Use a sharp knife to slice the Avocado BLT Sandwich in half diagonally. Secure each half with toothpicks if needed.

Enjoy:
- Serve the Avocado BLT Sandwich immediately as a delicious and satisfying meal.

This Avocado BLT Sandwich is a delightful twist on the classic BLT, adding creamy avocado for an extra layer of flavor and texture. The combination of crispy bacon, ripe avocado, fresh tomato, and lettuce creates a well-balanced and tasty sandwich. Enjoy this upgraded version of the classic BLT!

Chicken Avocado Burger

Ingredients:

For the Chicken Patties:

- 1 pound ground chicken
- 1/2 cup breadcrumbs
- 1/4 cup grated Parmesan cheese
- 1/4 cup red onion, finely chopped
- 2 cloves garlic, minced
- 1 teaspoon dried oregano
- Salt and black pepper to taste
- Cooking oil for grilling

For the Avocado Spread:

- 2 ripe avocados, peeled and pitted
- 1 tablespoon lime juice
- 1/4 cup fresh cilantro, chopped
- Salt and black pepper to taste

For Assembling:

- Burger buns
- Lettuce leaves
- Tomato slices
- Red onion slices
- Swiss or your favorite cheese (optional)

Instructions:

Prepare Chicken Patties:
- In a mixing bowl, combine ground chicken, breadcrumbs, grated Parmesan cheese, finely chopped red onion, minced garlic, dried oregano, salt, and black pepper. Mix until well combined.
- Divide the mixture into equal portions and shape them into burger patties.

Grill Patties:
- Preheat a grill or grill pan over medium-high heat. Brush the patties with cooking oil and grill for 5-7 minutes per side or until fully cooked.

Make Avocado Spread:
- In a bowl, mash the ripe avocados. Add lime juice, chopped cilantro, salt, and black pepper. Mix well to create a smooth avocado spread.

Assemble Burgers:
- Toast the burger buns if desired. Spread a generous layer of the avocado mixture on the bottom half of each bun.
- Place a grilled chicken patty on top of the avocado spread.
- Add lettuce leaves, tomato slices, and red onion slices. If desired, add a slice of Swiss or your favorite cheese.
- Top with the other half of the bun.

Serve:
- Serve the Chicken Avocado Burgers immediately, and enjoy!

These Chicken Avocado Burgers offer a flavorful and juicy twist to the classic burger by incorporating ground chicken and a creamy avocado spread. With the combination of grilled chicken, fresh veggies, and the rich taste of avocado, this burger is a delicious and healthier option. Enjoy the satisfying flavors in every bite!

Vegetarian Avocado Panini

Ingredients:

- 8 slices whole grain bread
- 2 ripe avocados, peeled, pitted, and sliced
- 1 cup baby spinach leaves
- 1 large tomato, sliced
- 1/2 cup red onion, thinly sliced
- 1/2 cup feta cheese, crumbled
- 1/4 cup fresh basil leaves
- Olive oil or cooking spray for grilling

Optional Sauce:

- 1/4 cup Greek yogurt or mayonnaise
- 1 tablespoon Dijon mustard
- 1 clove garlic, minced
- Salt and black pepper to taste

Instructions:

Preheat Panini Press or Grill Pan:
- Preheat the panini press or grill pan.

Prepare Optional Sauce (if using):
- In a small bowl, mix together Greek yogurt or mayonnaise, Dijon mustard, minced garlic, salt, and black pepper. Set aside.

Assemble Panini:
- Lay out 8 slices of whole grain bread.
- On four slices, evenly distribute avocado slices, baby spinach leaves, tomato slices, red onion slices, feta cheese, and fresh basil leaves.

Optional Sauce (if using):
- If using the optional sauce, spread a thin layer on the other four slices of bread.

Create Sandwiches:
- Place the slices with the sauce on top of the slices with the vegetables, creating four sandwiches.

Grill Panini:
- Brush the outside of each sandwich with olive oil or cooking spray.
- Grill the sandwiches in the panini press or grill pan until the bread is toasted, and the filling is heated through (about 3-5 minutes).

Serve:
- Cut the Vegetarian Avocado Panini in half and serve immediately.

Enjoy:
- Enjoy this flavorful and satisfying vegetarian panini with the goodness of avocado, veggies, and optional sauce!

This Vegetarian Avocado Panini is a delightful and healthy sandwich option, filled with the creamy texture of avocado, fresh veggies, and the tangy kick of feta cheese. Whether you enjoy it as a quick lunch or a light dinner, this panini is sure to please your taste buds. Customize with your favorite sauce or additional veggies for added variety!

Soups and Stews:

Chilled Avocado Soup

Ingredients:

- 3 ripe avocados, peeled and pitted
- 2 cucumbers, peeled and diced
- 1/2 red onion, diced
- 2 cloves garlic, minced
- 1 jalapeño, seeds removed and diced (optional for heat)
- 2 cups vegetable broth, chilled
- 1 cup plain Greek yogurt or coconut yogurt
- 1/4 cup fresh cilantro, chopped
- 1/4 cup fresh mint, chopped
- 2 tablespoons lime juice
- Salt and black pepper to taste
- Ice cubes (optional, for serving)
- Sliced radishes, cherry tomatoes, and extra herbs for garnish

Instructions:

Prepare Ingredients:
- Peel and pit the avocados. Peel and dice the cucumbers. Dice the red onion, mince the garlic, and dice the jalapeño.

Blend Ingredients:
- In a blender, combine avocados, cucumbers, red onion, garlic, jalapeño (if using), chilled vegetable broth, Greek yogurt, cilantro, mint, lime juice, salt, and black pepper. Blend until smooth and creamy.

Chill:
- Transfer the soup to a large bowl and refrigerate for at least 2 hours to chill thoroughly.

Serve:
- Ladle the chilled avocado soup into bowls. If desired, add ice cubes to each bowl for extra chill.

Garnish:
- Garnish the soup with sliced radishes, cherry tomatoes, and additional herbs.

Enjoy:

- Serve and enjoy this refreshing Chilled Avocado Soup as a light and flavorful appetizer or refreshing summer dish.

This Chilled Avocado Soup is a refreshing and creamy option for warm days. Packed with the goodness of avocados, cucumbers, and herbs, it's a delightful blend of flavors. The addition of Greek yogurt provides a creamy texture, while the lime juice adds a zesty kick. Enjoy this chilled soup as a light and nutritious meal!

Chicken Avocado Lime Soup

Ingredients:

- 1 pound boneless, skinless chicken breasts
- 1 tablespoon olive oil
- 1 large onion, diced
- 3 cloves garlic, minced
- 1 teaspoon ground cumin
- 1 teaspoon chili powder
- 1/2 teaspoon paprika
- 6 cups chicken broth
- 1 can (14 oz) diced tomatoes, undrained
- 1 can (15 oz) black beans, drained and rinsed
- 1 cup corn kernels (fresh, frozen, or canned)
- Juice of 2 limes
- Salt and black pepper to taste
- 2 avocados, peeled, pitted, and diced
- Fresh cilantro, chopped (for garnish)
- Sour cream or Greek yogurt (optional, for serving)

Instructions:

Cook Chicken:
- In a large pot, heat olive oil over medium heat. Add chicken breasts and cook until browned on both sides. Remove and set aside.

Sauté Aromatics:
- In the same pot, add diced onions and cook until softened. Add minced garlic, ground cumin, chili powder, and paprika. Sauté for an additional 1-2 minutes.

Add Broth and Tomatoes:
- Pour in chicken broth and diced tomatoes (undrained). Bring to a simmer.

Shred Chicken:
- Shred the cooked chicken using two forks. Add the shredded chicken back into the pot.

Add Beans and Corn:
- Stir in black beans and corn. Simmer for about 10-15 minutes until flavors meld.

Season with Lime Juice:
- Squeeze the juice of 2 limes into the soup. Season with salt and black pepper to taste.

Add Avocado:
- Just before serving, add diced avocados to the soup.

Garnish and Serve:
- Ladle the Chicken Avocado Lime Soup into bowls. Garnish with chopped cilantro. Optionally, add a dollop of sour cream or Greek yogurt.

Enjoy:
- Serve immediately and enjoy this flavorful and comforting Chicken Avocado Lime Soup.

This Chicken Avocado Lime Soup is a hearty and satisfying dish with a burst of fresh flavors. The combination of shredded chicken, creamy avocado, and zesty lime creates a comforting soup perfect for any season. Garnish with your favorite toppings and enjoy a delicious bowl of homemade goodness!

Black Bean and Avocado Chili

Ingredients:

- 1 tablespoon olive oil
- 1 large onion, diced
- 3 cloves garlic, minced
- 1 bell pepper, diced (any color)
- 1 zucchini, diced
- 1 carrot, diced
- 2 teaspoons ground cumin
- 1 teaspoon chili powder
- 1 teaspoon smoked paprika
- 1 can (14 oz) diced tomatoes, undrained
- 2 cans (15 oz each) black beans, drained and rinsed
- 1 can (15 oz) corn kernels, drained
- 4 cups vegetable broth
- Salt and black pepper to taste
- 1 avocado, peeled, pitted, and diced
- Fresh cilantro, chopped (for garnish)
- Lime wedges (for serving)
- Sour cream or Greek yogurt (optional, for serving)

Instructions:

Sauté Vegetables:
- In a large pot, heat olive oil over medium heat. Add diced onion, garlic, bell pepper, zucchini, and carrot. Sauté until vegetables are softened.

Add Spices:
- Add ground cumin, chili powder, and smoked paprika to the sautéed vegetables. Stir well to coat the vegetables in the spices.

Incorporate Tomatoes and Beans:
- Pour in the diced tomatoes (undrained), black beans, and corn. Stir to combine.

Pour in Broth:
- Add vegetable broth to the pot. Bring the mixture to a simmer.

Season and Simmer:
- Season the chili with salt and black pepper to taste. Allow the chili to simmer for 20-25 minutes to let the flavors meld.

Add Avocado:

- Just before serving, stir in the diced avocado. This ensures that the avocado stays fresh and creamy.

Garnish and Serve:
- Ladle the Black Bean and Avocado Chili into bowls. Garnish with chopped cilantro. Serve with lime wedges and, if desired, a dollop of sour cream or Greek yogurt.

Enjoy:
- Serve and savor this delicious and nutritious Black Bean and Avocado Chili.

This Black Bean and Avocado Chili is a hearty and flavorful dish that combines the richness of black beans, the creaminess of avocado, and a blend of aromatic spices. Enjoy the comforting warmth of this chili topped with fresh garnishes for a satisfying and wholesome meal!

Avocado and Corn Chowder

Ingredients:

- 1 tablespoon olive oil
- 1 onion, diced
- 2 cloves garlic, minced
- 1 red bell pepper, diced
- 1 celery stalk, diced
- 3 cups corn kernels (fresh or frozen)
- 2 large potatoes, peeled and diced
- 4 cups vegetable broth
- 1 teaspoon ground cumin
- 1 teaspoon smoked paprika
- 1/2 teaspoon chili powder
- Salt and black pepper to taste
- 1 can (14 oz) coconut milk
- 2 ripe avocados, peeled, pitted, and diced
- Juice of 1 lime
- Fresh cilantro, chopped (for garnish)
- Red pepper flakes (optional, for extra heat)

Instructions:

Sauté Aromatics:
- In a large pot, heat olive oil over medium heat. Add diced onion, minced garlic, red bell pepper, and celery. Sauté until the vegetables are softened.

Add Corn and Potatoes:
- Add corn kernels and diced potatoes to the pot. Stir to combine with the sautéed vegetables.

Pour in Broth:
- Pour vegetable broth into the pot. Bring the mixture to a boil.

Season with Spices:
- Add ground cumin, smoked paprika, chili powder, salt, and black pepper to the pot. Stir well and reduce the heat to a simmer. Let it cook until the potatoes are tender.

Blend and Simmer:
- Use an immersion blender to partially blend the chowder, leaving some chunks for texture. If you don't have an immersion blender, transfer a portion of the chowder to a blender and blend until smooth before returning it to the pot.

Add Coconut Milk:

- Pour in the coconut milk, stirring to combine. Simmer for an additional 5-10 minutes to allow the flavors to meld.

Finish with Avocado:
- Just before serving, stir in diced avocados and lime juice. Adjust the seasoning if needed.

Garnish and Serve:
- Ladle the Avocado and Corn Chowder into bowls. Garnish with chopped cilantro and, if desired, red pepper flakes for extra heat.

Enjoy:
- Serve and enjoy this creamy and flavorful Avocado and Corn Chowder as a comforting and nutritious meal.

This Avocado and Corn Chowder offers a delightful combination of creamy avocado, sweet corn, and aromatic spices. The addition of coconut milk provides richness, making it a satisfying and comforting soup. Garnish with fresh cilantro and red pepper flakes for a burst of flavor. Enjoy a bowl of this nourishing chowder!

Breakfast and Brunch:

Avocado Toast Variations

Classic Avocado Toast:

- Ingredients:
    - 1 slice whole-grain bread, toasted
    - 1 ripe avocado, mashed
    - Salt and black pepper to taste
    - Optional toppings: red pepper flakes, a drizzle of olive oil, or a squeeze of lemon juice

Tomato and Basil Avocado Toast:

- Ingredients:
    - 1 slice whole-grain bread, toasted
    - 1 ripe avocado, mashed
    - Sliced cherry tomatoes

- Fresh basil leaves
- Balsamic glaze or reduction (optional)
- Salt and black pepper to taste

Smoked Salmon Avocado Toast:

- Ingredients:
    - 1 slice whole-grain bread, toasted
    - 1 ripe avocado, mashed
    - Smoked salmon slices
    - Capers
    - Fresh dill
    - Lemon wedges
    - Salt and black pepper to taste

Poached Egg and Spinach Avocado Toast:

- Ingredients:
    - 1 slice whole-grain bread, toasted
    - 1 ripe avocado, mashed
    - Poached egg
    - Sautéed spinach
    - Red pepper flakes (optional)
    - Salt and black pepper to taste

Mediterranean Avocado Toast:

- Ingredients:
    - 1 slice whole-grain bread, toasted
    - 1 ripe avocado, mashed
    - Cherry tomatoes, halved
    - Cucumber slices
    - Kalamata olives, sliced
    - Feta cheese, crumbled
    - Olive oil drizzle
    - Salt and black pepper to taste

Pico de Gallo Avocado Toast:

- Ingredients:
    - 1 slice whole-grain bread, toasted

- 1 ripe avocado, mashed
- Homemade pico de gallo (tomatoes, onions, cilantro, lime juice)
- Jalapeño slices (optional)
- Salt and black pepper to taste

Everything Bagel Avocado Toast:

- Ingredients:
  - 1 slice whole-grain bread, toasted
  - 1 ripe avocado, mashed
  - Everything bagel seasoning
  - Radish slices
  - Microgreens or arugula
  - Salt and black pepper to taste

Goat Cheese and Honey Avocado Toast:

- Ingredients:
  - 1 slice whole-grain bread, toasted
  - 1 ripe avocado, mashed
  - Goat cheese crumbles
  - Drizzle of honey
  - Crushed red pepper flakes (optional)
  - Salt and black pepper to taste

Avocado and Hummus Toast:

- Ingredients:
  - 1 slice whole-grain bread, toasted
  - 1 ripe avocado, mashed
  - Hummus
  - Cherry tomatoes, halved
  - Sprinkle of paprika
  - Salt and black pepper to taste

BLT Avocado Toast:

- Ingredients:
  - 1 slice whole-grain bread, toasted
  - 1 ripe avocado, mashed
  - Crispy bacon slices

- Lettuce leaves
- Tomato slices
- Salt and black pepper to taste

Instructions for Each Variation:

Prepare Toast:
- Toast a slice of whole-grain bread until golden brown.

Mash Avocado:
- Mash a ripe avocado and spread it evenly on the toasted bread.

Add Toppings:
- Add the specific toppings for each variation as listed above.

Season:
- Season with salt and black pepper to taste.

Enjoy:
- Enjoy your creative and delicious Avocado Toast variation!

Avocado and Spinach Omelette

Ingredients:

- 2 large eggs
- 1/4 cup milk (optional for a fluffier omelette)
- Salt and black pepper to taste
- 1 tablespoon olive oil or butter
- 1/2 cup fresh spinach, chopped
- 1/4 cup cherry tomatoes, halved
- 1/4 cup feta cheese, crumbled
- 1/2 avocado, sliced
- Fresh herbs (e.g., parsley or chives), chopped for garnish (optional)

Instructions:

Prepare Ingredients:
- Chop the fresh spinach, halve the cherry tomatoes, crumble the feta cheese, and slice the avocado.

Whisk Eggs:
- In a bowl, whisk together the eggs and milk (if using). Season with salt and black pepper.

Heat Pan:
- Heat olive oil or butter in a non-stick skillet over medium heat.

Sauté Spinach and Tomatoes:
- Add chopped spinach and halved cherry tomatoes to the pan. Sauté until the spinach wilts and tomatoes soften.

Pour Egg Mixture:
- Pour the whisked egg mixture over the sautéed spinach and tomatoes.

Add Feta Cheese:
- Sprinkle crumbled feta cheese evenly over the eggs.

Cook Omelette:
- Allow the omelette to cook undisturbed for a few moments until the edges set.

Fold Omelette:
- Gently lift the edges of the omelette with a spatula and tilt the pan to let any uncooked eggs flow to the edges. Once most of the eggs are set but still slightly runny on top, add sliced avocado on one side of the omelette.

Fold and Serve:
- Carefully fold the omelette in half, covering the avocado. Cook for an additional minute or until the eggs are fully cooked but still moist.

Garnish and Serve:

- Slide the omelette onto a plate. Garnish with fresh herbs if desired.

Enjoy:
- Serve the Avocado and Spinach Omelette hot and enjoy a delicious and nutritious breakfast or brunch!

This Avocado and Spinach Omelette is a wholesome and flavorful breakfast option. The combination of creamy avocado, savory feta cheese, and vibrant spinach creates a delightful omelette that is both satisfying and nutritious. Customize with your favorite herbs and enjoy a delicious start to your day!

Avocado Pancakes

Ingredients:

- 1 ripe avocado, peeled and pitted
- 1 cup all-purpose flour
- 1 tablespoon sugar
- 1 teaspoon baking powder
- 1/2 teaspoon baking soda
- 1/4 teaspoon salt
- 1 cup buttermilk
- 1 large egg
- 2 tablespoons unsalted butter, melted
- 1 teaspoon vanilla extract
- Cooking oil or butter for greasing the pan
- Maple syrup and sliced strawberries for serving (optional)

Instructions:

Prepare Avocado:
- In a bowl, mash the ripe avocado until smooth.

Mix Dry Ingredients:
- In a separate large bowl, whisk together the all-purpose flour, sugar, baking powder, baking soda, and salt.

Combine Wet Ingredients:
- To the mashed avocado, add buttermilk, egg, melted butter, and vanilla extract. Mix until well combined.

Make Batter:
- Pour the wet ingredients into the bowl with the dry ingredients. Stir until just combined. Do not overmix; some lumps are okay.

Heat Pan:
- Heat a griddle or non-stick skillet over medium heat. Lightly grease with cooking oil or butter.

Cook Pancakes:
- Pour 1/4 cup of batter onto the hot griddle for each pancake. Cook until bubbles form on the surface, then flip and cook until the other side is golden brown.

Repeat:
- Repeat the process with the remaining batter, adding more oil or butter to the pan as needed.

Serve:

- Stack the Avocado Pancakes on a plate. Serve with maple syrup and sliced strawberries if desired.

Enjoy:
- Enjoy these fluffy and green-tinted pancakes as a unique and delicious breakfast treat!

These Avocado Pancakes are a creative twist on classic pancakes, adding the creamy goodness of avocado to the mix. The result is a stack of fluffy, green-tinted pancakes that are not only visually appealing but also deliciously moist. Top them with maple syrup and fresh berries for a delightful breakfast or brunch experience.

Breakfast Burrito with Avocado

Ingredients:

- 1 large tortilla (flour or whole grain)
- 2 large eggs, scrambled
- 1/4 cup black beans, drained and rinsed
- 1/4 cup diced tomatoes
- 1/4 cup diced bell peppers (any color)
- 2 tablespoons diced red onion
- 1/4 cup shredded cheddar cheese
- 1/2 avocado, sliced
- Fresh cilantro, chopped (for garnish)
- Salt and black pepper to taste
- Hot sauce or salsa (optional)
- Cooking oil for scrambling eggs

Instructions:

Prepare Ingredients:
- Scramble the eggs and season with salt and black pepper. Dice the tomatoes, bell peppers, red onion, and avocado.

Cook Scrambled Eggs:
- Heat a skillet over medium heat, add a small amount of cooking oil, and scramble the eggs until cooked to your liking.

Warm Tortilla:
- In the same skillet or on a separate griddle, warm the tortilla until pliable.

Assemble Burrito:
- Place the warmed tortilla on a flat surface. In the center of the tortilla, layer the scrambled eggs, black beans, diced tomatoes, bell peppers, red onion, shredded cheddar cheese, and sliced avocado.

Fold and Roll:
- Fold the sides of the tortilla over the filling, and then roll it from the bottom to create a burrito.

Serve:
- Place the Breakfast Burrito on a plate, seam side down. If desired, drizzle with hot sauce or serve with salsa on the side.

Garnish:
- Garnish with chopped cilantro for a burst of freshness.

Enjoy:

- Enjoy this hearty and satisfying Breakfast Burrito with Avocado for a delicious start to your day!

This Breakfast Burrito with Avocado is a perfect combination of protein-packed eggs, creamy avocado, and a variety of fresh vegetables. It's a quick and customizable breakfast option that provides a balance of flavors and textures. Feel free to add your favorite ingredients or condiments to suit your taste preferences.

Dressings and Sauces:

Creamy Avocado Caesar Dressing

Ingredients:

- 1 ripe avocado, peeled and pitted
- 1/4 cup grated Parmesan cheese
- 2 tablespoons fresh lemon juice
- 2 tablespoons mayonnaise
- 2 cloves garlic, minced
- 1 teaspoon Dijon mustard
- 1/4 cup extra-virgin olive oil
- Salt and black pepper to taste
- Water (as needed to adjust consistency)

Instructions:

Blend Avocado:
- In a blender or food processor, combine the ripe avocado, grated Parmesan cheese, fresh lemon juice, mayonnaise, minced garlic, and Dijon mustard.

Blend until Smooth:
- Blend the ingredients until smooth and creamy.

Add Olive Oil:
- With the blender or food processor running, gradually drizzle in the extra-virgin olive oil until well incorporated.

Adjust Consistency:
- If the dressing is too thick, add water a tablespoon at a time until you reach your desired consistency. Blend again to combine.

Season:
- Season the dressing with salt and black pepper to taste. Blend once more to ensure even seasoning.

Taste and Adjust:
- Taste the dressing and adjust the lemon juice, salt, or pepper as needed.

Transfer and Store:
- Transfer the Creamy Avocado Caesar Dressing to a jar or container. Seal tightly and refrigerate until ready to use.

Serve:
- Serve the dressing over your favorite Caesar salad or use it as a flavorful dip.

Enjoy:

- Enjoy the rich and creamy goodness of this homemade Avocado Caesar Dressing!

This Creamy Avocado Caesar Dressing is a healthier and avocado-rich alternative to traditional Caesar dressings. The combination of creamy avocado, Parmesan cheese, and zesty lemon creates a deliciously indulgent dressing perfect for drizzling over salads or as a dip. Customize the consistency and seasonings to suit your taste preferences.

Avocado Chimichurri Sauce

Ingredients:

- 1 ripe avocado, peeled and pitted
- 1 cup fresh parsley, finely chopped
- 1/4 cup fresh cilantro, finely chopped
- 3 cloves garlic, minced
- 1/4 cup red wine vinegar
- 1/2 cup extra-virgin olive oil
- 1 teaspoon dried oregano
- 1 teaspoon ground cumin
- 1/2 teaspoon red pepper flakes (adjust to taste)
- Salt and black pepper to taste
- Juice of 1 lime

Instructions:

Prepare Avocado:
- In a bowl, mash the ripe avocado until smooth.

Chop Herbs:
- Finely chop the fresh parsley and cilantro.

Combine Ingredients:
- In a bowl, combine the mashed avocado, chopped parsley, chopped cilantro, minced garlic, red wine vinegar, extra-virgin olive oil, dried oregano, ground cumin, red pepper flakes, salt, black pepper, and lime juice.

Mix Thoroughly:
- Mix the ingredients thoroughly until well combined.

Adjust Seasoning:
- Taste the chimichurri sauce and adjust the salt, pepper, or red pepper flakes as needed to suit your taste.

Serve or Refrigerate:
- Serve the Avocado Chimichurri Sauce immediately as a condiment for grilled meats, vegetables, or as a dip. Alternatively, refrigerate it in a sealed container until ready to use.

Enjoy:
- Enjoy the rich and flavorful Avocado Chimichurri Sauce with your favorite dishes!

This Avocado Chimichurri Sauce is a delightful twist on the classic chimichurri, incorporating the creamy texture of avocado into the vibrant herb and spice mixture. Whether used as a marinade, dressing, or condiment, this sauce adds a burst of freshness and flavor to grilled meats, roasted vegetables, or as a dip for crusty bread. Adjust the spice levels to your liking and savor the rich taste of avocado in every bite.

Avocado Lime Crema

Ingredients:

- 1 ripe avocado, peeled and pitted
- 1/2 cup sour cream or Greek yogurt
- 1-2 tablespoons fresh lime juice (adjust to taste)
- 1 clove garlic, minced
- Salt and black pepper to taste
- Fresh cilantro, chopped (optional, for garnish)

Instructions:

Prepare Avocado:
- In a bowl, mash the ripe avocado until smooth.

Combine Ingredients:
- Add sour cream or Greek yogurt, fresh lime juice, minced garlic, salt, and black pepper to the mashed avocado.

Mix Thoroughly:
- Mix the ingredients thoroughly until well combined. Adjust lime juice, salt, or pepper to taste.

Blend for Creaminess (Optional):
- For an extra smooth and creamy texture, you can use a blender or food processor to blend the ingredients until the crema reaches your desired consistency.

Garnish (Optional):
- Garnish the Avocado Lime Crema with chopped fresh cilantro for a burst of flavor and color.

Serve:
- Serve the crema immediately as a topping for tacos, enchiladas, grilled meats, or as a dip for vegetables.

Store:
- If not serving immediately, store the Avocado Lime Crema in a sealed container in the refrigerator. Use within a day or two for the best freshness.

Enjoy:
- Enjoy the creamy and zesty goodness of this Avocado Lime Crema with your favorite dishes!

This Avocado Lime Crema is a versatile and flavorful topping that adds a creamy and citrusy kick to a variety of dishes. Use it as a condiment for Mexican-inspired meals, drizzle it over grilled proteins, or serve it as a refreshing dip. The combination of avocado and lime creates a deliciously smooth and tangy crema that elevates the flavors of your favorite dishes.

Desserts:
Avocado Chocolate Mousse

Ingredients:

- 2 ripe avocados, peeled and pitted
- 1/2 cup unsweetened cocoa powder
- 1/2 cup maple syrup or honey (adjust to taste)
- 1/4 cup almond milk or any milk of choice
- 1 teaspoon vanilla extract
- A pinch of salt
- Optional toppings: whipped cream, berries, chopped nuts

Instructions:

Prepare Avocado:
- In a blender or food processor, add the ripe avocados.

Add Cocoa Powder:
- Add unsweetened cocoa powder to the blender.

Sweeten with Maple Syrup:
- Pour in the maple syrup or honey for sweetness. Adjust the amount to suit your taste preferences.

Add Liquid and Flavorings:
- Pour in the almond milk, add vanilla extract, and a pinch of salt.

Blend Until Smooth:
- Blend all the ingredients until the mixture is smooth and creamy. Scrape down the sides of the blender or food processor as needed.

Adjust Sweetness:
- Taste the chocolate mousse and adjust the sweetness if necessary by adding more maple syrup or honey.

Chill:
- Transfer the chocolate mousse to a bowl or individual serving glasses. Cover and refrigerate for at least 2 hours to allow the mousse to set.

Serve:
- Once chilled, serve the Avocado Chocolate Mousse on its own or with optional toppings like whipped cream, berries, or chopped nuts.

Enjoy:
- Indulge in this rich and creamy Avocado Chocolate Mousse as a delicious and healthier dessert option!

This Avocado Chocolate Mousse is a decadent and guilt-free treat that combines the creamy texture of avocados with the richness of chocolate. The result is a smooth and luscious mousse that's easy to make and delightful to eat. Customize the sweetness to your liking and enjoy this healthier dessert option with your favorite toppings.

Avocado Lime Cheesecake Bars

Crust Ingredients:

- 1 1/2 cups graham cracker crumbs
- 1/2 cup unsalted butter, melted
- 1/4 cup granulated sugar

Filling Ingredients:

- 3 ripe avocados, peeled and pitted
- 1 cup cream cheese, softened
- 1 cup granulated sugar
- 3 large eggs
- Zest of 2 limes
- 1/3 cup fresh lime juice
- 1 teaspoon vanilla extract

Topping (Optional):

- Whipped cream
- Lime slices or zest for garnish

Instructions:

Preheat Oven:
- Preheat your oven to 325°F (163°C). Grease a 9x9-inch (23x23 cm) baking pan or line it with parchment paper, leaving an overhang for easy removal.

Prepare Crust:
- In a bowl, combine graham cracker crumbs, melted butter, and granulated sugar. Press the mixture evenly into the bottom of the prepared pan.

Bake Crust:
- Bake the crust in the preheated oven for about 10 minutes or until set. Remove from the oven and let it cool while you prepare the filling.

Prepare Filling:
- In a blender or food processor, combine ripe avocados, softened cream cheese, granulated sugar, eggs, lime zest, lime juice, and vanilla extract. Blend until smooth and creamy.

Pour over Crust:
- Pour the avocado lime filling over the cooled crust, spreading it evenly.

Bake Cheesecake Bars:

- Bake in the preheated oven for 25-30 minutes or until the center is set. The edges should be slightly golden. Allow it to cool completely in the pan.

Chill:
- Refrigerate the cheesecake bars for at least 4 hours or overnight to allow them to set.

Slice:
- Once chilled and set, use the parchment paper overhang to lift the cheesecake out of the pan. Cut into squares or bars.

Serve:
- Optional: Top each bar with a dollop of whipped cream and garnish with lime slices or zest.

Enjoy:
- Serve and enjoy these refreshing Avocado Lime Cheesecake Bars as a delightful dessert!

These Avocado Lime Cheesecake Bars are a unique and refreshing twist on traditional cheesecake. The creamy avocado and zesty lime create a deliciously tangy flavor, while the graham cracker crust adds a perfect crunch. Top with whipped cream and lime for a beautiful presentation and extra burst of freshness.

Avocado Key Lime Pie

Crust Ingredients:

- 1 1/2 cups graham cracker crumbs
- 1/2 cup unsalted butter, melted
- 1/4 cup granulated sugar

Filling Ingredients:

- 3 ripe avocados, peeled and pitted
- 1 cup sweetened condensed milk
- 1/2 cup sour cream
- 1/2 cup fresh key lime juice
- Zest of 2 key limes
- 3 large egg yolks
- 1 teaspoon vanilla extract

Topping (Optional):

- Whipped cream
- Key lime slices or zest for garnish

Instructions:

Preheat Oven:
- Preheat your oven to 350°F (177°C). Grease a 9-inch (23 cm) pie dish.

Prepare Crust:
- In a bowl, combine graham cracker crumbs, melted butter, and granulated sugar. Press the mixture into the bottom and up the sides of the pie dish to form the crust.

Bake Crust:
- Bake the crust in the preheated oven for about 10 minutes or until it is set and lightly golden. Remove from the oven and let it cool while you prepare the filling.

Prepare Filling:
- In a blender or food processor, combine ripe avocados, sweetened condensed milk, sour cream, key lime juice, lime zest, egg yolks, and vanilla extract. Blend until smooth and creamy.

Pour into Crust:
- Pour the avocado key lime filling into the cooled crust, spreading it evenly.

Bake Pie:
- Bake in the preheated oven for 15-20 minutes or until the center is set. The edges should be slightly firm. Allow the pie to cool to room temperature.

Chill:
- Refrigerate the pie for at least 4 hours or overnight to allow it to set.

Top and Garnish:
- Optional: Top the chilled pie with whipped cream and garnish with key lime slices or zest.

Serve:
- Slice and serve this delightful Avocado Key Lime Pie.

Enjoy:
- Enjoy the creamy and tangy goodness of this unique Avocado Key Lime Pie!

This Avocado Key Lime Pie offers a creamy and luscious filling with the added richness of ripe avocados. The combination of sweetened condensed milk, key lime juice, and a graham cracker crust creates a deliciously refreshing dessert. Top it with whipped cream and key lime garnish for a perfect finish. Savor each bite of this tropical-inspired pie!

Avocado Coconut Ice Cream

Ingredients:

- 2 ripe avocados, peeled and pitted
- 1 can (13.5 oz) coconut milk (full-fat)
- 1/2 cup coconut cream
- 1/2 cup honey or maple syrup (adjust to taste)
- 1 teaspoon vanilla extract
- A pinch of salt
- Shredded coconut for garnish (optional)

Instructions:

Prepare Avocado:
- In a blender or food processor, combine the ripe avocados.

Add Coconut Milk and Cream:
- Add the coconut milk and coconut cream to the blender.

Sweeten and Flavor:
- Pour in honey or maple syrup, add vanilla extract, and a pinch of salt.

Blend until Smooth:
- Blend all the ingredients until the mixture is smooth and well combined. Scrape down the sides of the blender or food processor as needed.

Taste and Adjust:
- Taste the mixture and adjust the sweetness or vanilla extract if necessary.

Chill:
- Refrigerate the mixture for at least 2 hours to chill it thoroughly.

Churn Ice Cream:
- Transfer the chilled mixture to an ice cream maker and churn according to the manufacturer's instructions until it reaches a soft-serve consistency.

Freeze:
- Transfer the churned ice cream to a lidded container. Smooth the top with a spatula, cover, and freeze for at least 4 hours or until firm.

Serve:
- Scoop the Avocado Coconut Ice Cream into bowls or cones.

Garnish (Optional):
- Optional: Garnish with shredded coconut for an extra touch of flavor and texture.

Enjoy:

- Indulge in this creamy and tropical Avocado Coconut Ice Cream as a delightful and refreshing treat!

This Avocado Coconut Ice Cream combines the creamy texture of ripe avocados with the rich and tropical flavor of coconut. It's a dairy-free and naturally sweetened frozen dessert that's both satisfying and refreshing. Enjoy a scoop or two on a hot day for a cool and indulgent treat!

Drinks:

Avocado Smoothie

Ingredients:

- 1 ripe avocado, peeled and pitted
- 1 banana, peeled
- 1 cup spinach leaves (fresh or frozen)
- 1/2 cup Greek yogurt or dairy-free alternative
- 1 cup unsweetened almond milk or any milk of choice
- 1 tablespoon honey or maple syrup (optional, for sweetness)
- Ice cubes (optional)

Optional Add-ins:

- 1 tablespoon chia seeds
- 1/2 cup pineapple chunks (fresh or frozen)
- 1 tablespoon flaxseeds
- Protein powder for an added protein boost

Instructions:

Prepare Ingredients:
- Ensure the avocado is ripe, and the banana is peeled.

Combine in Blender:
- In a blender, combine the ripe avocado, banana, spinach leaves, Greek yogurt, almond milk, and honey (if using).

Blend Until Smooth:
- Blend the ingredients until smooth and creamy. If the smoothie is too thick, you can add more almond milk to achieve your desired consistency.

Taste and Adjust:
- Taste the smoothie and add more honey if additional sweetness is desired.

Optional Add-ins:
- If you'd like to incorporate optional add-ins like chia seeds, pineapple chunks, flaxseeds, or protein powder, add them to the blender and blend until well combined.

Ice Cubes (Optional):
- If you prefer a colder smoothie, add a handful of ice cubes and blend until smooth.

Pour and Serve:
- Pour the Avocado Smoothie into glasses.

Garnish (Optional):
- Optional: Garnish with a slice of avocado or a sprinkle of chia seeds on top for presentation.

Enjoy:
- Enjoy this nutritious and creamy Avocado Smoothie as a refreshing and satisfying beverage!

This Avocado Smoothie is a nutrient-packed and delicious way to incorporate avocado into your diet. The combination of creamy avocado, banana, and spinach creates a smooth and refreshing drink that can be enjoyed for breakfast, as a snack, or post-workout. Feel free to customize the smoothie with your favorite add-ins for an extra boost of flavor and nutrition.

Avocado Margarita

Ingredients:

- 2 ripe avocados, peeled and pitted
- 1 cup silver tequila
- 1/2 cup triple sec or orange liqueur
- 1/2 cup fresh lime juice
- 1/4 cup agave syrup or simple syrup (adjust to taste)
- Ice cubes
- Salt or Tajin for rimming glasses (optional)
- Lime slices for garnish (optional)

Instructions:

Prepare Avocado:
- Ensure the avocados are ripe and peeled.

Rim Glasses (Optional):
- If desired, moisten the rims of the glasses with a lime wedge and dip them into salt or Tajin for a salty or spicy rim.

Blend Ingredients:
- In a blender, combine ripe avocados, silver tequila, triple sec, fresh lime juice, and agave syrup.

Add Ice and Blend:
- Add ice cubes to the blender. Blend all the ingredients until smooth and well combined.

Taste and Adjust:
- Taste the margarita and adjust the sweetness by adding more agave syrup if needed.

Pour into Glasses:
- Pour the Avocado Margarita into prepared glasses.

Garnish (Optional):
- Optional: Garnish with lime slices on the rim or floating in the margarita for an extra touch of freshness.

Serve:
- Serve the Avocado Margarita immediately.

Enjoy:
- Sip and enjoy this creamy and flavorful Avocado Margarita for a unique twist on the classic cocktail!

This Avocado Margarita is a creamy and indulgent variation of the classic margarita, blending the richness of ripe avocados with the bold flavors of tequila and lime. Whether you're lounging by the pool or hosting a gathering, this unique cocktail is sure to impress with its smooth texture and delightful taste. Cheers!

Avocado Matcha Latte

Ingredients:

- 1 ripe avocado, peeled and pitted
- 1 teaspoon matcha powder
- 1 cup almond milk or any milk of choice
- 1-2 tablespoons honey or maple syrup (adjust to taste)
- Ice cubes (optional)
- Matcha powder for dusting (optional)

Instructions:

Prepare Avocado:
- Ensure the avocado is ripe and peeled.

Blend Ingredients:
- In a blender, combine the ripe avocado, matcha powder, almond milk, and honey (or maple syrup).

Blend Until Smooth:
- Blend all the ingredients until smooth and well combined.

Taste and Adjust:
- Taste the Avocado Matcha Latte and adjust the sweetness by adding more honey or maple syrup if desired.

Optional Ice Cubes:
- If you prefer a colder drink, add ice cubes to the blender and blend until the ice is crushed and the latte is chilled.

Pour into a Glass:
- Pour the Avocado Matcha Latte into a glass.

Optional Dusting:
- Optional: Dust the top of the latte with a sprinkle of matcha powder for presentation.

Stir (Optional):
- If the matcha settles at the bottom, give the latte a gentle stir with a spoon.

Serve:
- Serve the Avocado Matcha Latte immediately.

Enjoy:
- Sip and enjoy this creamy and vibrant Avocado Matcha Latte as a refreshing and nutritious beverage!

This Avocado Matcha Latte combines the creamy texture of ripe avocados with the earthy and vibrant flavors of matcha green tea. It's a delightful and nutritious drink that provides a boost of energy and antioxidants. Whether enjoyed in the morning or as an afternoon pick-me-up, this latte offers a unique twist on the traditional matcha drink.

Avocado and Berry Smoothie Bowl

Ingredients:

- 1 ripe avocado, peeled and pitted
- 1 cup mixed berries (strawberries, blueberries, raspberries)
- 1 banana, peeled and frozen
- 1/2 cup Greek yogurt or dairy-free alternative
- 1/2 cup almond milk or any milk of choice
- 1 tablespoon honey or maple syrup (optional, for sweetness)
- Toppings: sliced strawberries, blueberries, granola, chia seeds, coconut flakes

Instructions:

Prepare Ingredients:
- Ensure the avocado is ripe, peel and pit it. Peel and freeze the banana ahead of time.

Blend Smoothie Base:
- In a blender, combine the ripe avocado, mixed berries, frozen banana, Greek yogurt, almond milk, and honey (if using).

Blend Until Smooth:
- Blend all the ingredients until smooth and creamy. Add more almond milk if needed to achieve the desired consistency.

Taste and Adjust:
- Taste the smoothie and add more honey if additional sweetness is desired.

Pour into a Bowl:
- Pour the Avocado and Berry Smoothie into a bowl.

Add Toppings:
- Arrange sliced strawberries, blueberries, granola, chia seeds, and coconut flakes on top of the smoothie.

Drizzle (Optional):
- Optional: Drizzle with additional honey or maple syrup for extra sweetness.

Serve:
- Serve the Avocado and Berry Smoothie Bowl immediately.

Enjoy:
- Enjoy this nutritious and visually appealing smoothie bowl as a satisfying and wholesome breakfast or snack!

This Avocado and Berry Smoothie Bowl offers a delicious and vibrant combination of creamy avocado and sweet mixed berries. Topped with a variety of textures and flavors, it provides a nutritious and visually appealing breakfast or snack. Customize the toppings based on your preferences and enjoy this refreshing bowl of goodness!